01010111 01101001 01101100 01101100 01101011
01101111 01101101 01101101 01100101 01101110
00100000 01101001 01101110 00100000 01100100
01100101 01110010 00100000 01100111 01100001
01110100 01100010 01101001 01111000 00100000

01010111 01101001 01101100 01101100 01101011
01101111 01101101 01101101 01100101 01101110
00100000 01101001 01101110 00100000 01100100
01100101 01110010 00100000 01100111 01100001
01110100 01100010 01101001 01111000 00100000

01010111 01101001 01101100 01101100 01101011
01101111 01101101 01101101 01100101 01101110
00100000 01101001 01101110 00100000 01100100
01100101 01110010 00100000 01100111 01100001
01110100 01100010 01101001 01111000 00100000

01010111 01101001 01101100 01101100 01101011
01101111 01101101 01101101 01100101 01101110
00100000 01101001 01101110 00100000 01100100
01100101 01110010 00100000 01100111 01100001
01110100 01100010 01101001 01111000 00100000

01010111 01101001 01101100 01101100 01101011
01101111 01101101 01101101 01100101 01101110
00100000 01101001 01101110 00100000 01100100
01100101 01110010 00100000 01100111 01100001
01110100 01100010 01101001 01111000 00100000

Dennis Hans Ladener

Philosophy made in Germany

THE DATA WORLD
THEORY 2.0

Freethinkers

1st edition
© 2020 Dennis Hans Ladener
(dladener@googlemail.com)

Production and publishing: BoD - Books on Demand, Norderstedt.

ISBN: 9783751979467

*"Information is what informs.
So that from which data can be
derived. No materialism that does
not admit this can survive today. "
~ Norbert Wiener*

Dennis Hans Ladener,

born May 11th, 1990 in Cologne/Germany, is a German philosopher and writer who, at the young age of only **29**, managed to bring *eighteen*  "philosophical non-fiction books" to market on his own.

The focus of his work, as well as his thinking, is based on the philosophy of the brilliant German philosopher Arthur Schopenhauer *(* February 22, 1788 in Danzig; † September 21, 1860 Frankfurt am Main)*.

Since his main work *"The world as will and idea"*,

always had the greatest source of inspiration for himself.

"I must have always been a little weird, and even as a child I spent a lot of time thinking about the world. Fantasy, imagination and a strong natural curiosity have always been my most loyal companions. "

"The secret behind why I have become what I am is probably hidden in the fact that I have always avoided becoming an" adult "!"

In 2011, he successfully completed his three-year training as a ***"Specialist for protection and security".***

From now on he could concentrate fully on his "personal study" of philosophy.

"At the age of 20, I finally fell in love with philosophy and finally with Arthur Schopenhauer's world of thought."

"It was a long, lonely and rocky road. But I've never regretted going with him! "

Synopsis

Introduction

Humans have always had the longing to escape to other worlds, which initially began with stories around the campfire, but now computers and video games make it possible for us as well Movie and TV. In between were books, plays, gladiatorial games and the like.

These days, however, they play a rather subordinate role than with the as our century progressed, the worlds into which we can escape have also become more and more advanced.

In a world with *computers, Playstation and Co*, there is hardly any space left for the retreats of past generations. We have long been dominated by a world of data and simulations, and this is also thankfully accepted by our society, which one can see in games like ***The Sims, Grand Theft Auto or World of Warcraft*** can clearly see.

What used to be considered impossible or as Witchcraft had been dismissed is now something completely every day for us and is perceived as completely normal and natural.

> ***No matter where we look, people are in digital worlds.***

The development of Smartphones, tablets and portable game consoles make this very easy for us. Everywhere you see screens flashing to capture their owners in a world full of data.

> ***"You ask yourself who owns whom here?"***

But what if I told you now that our entire universe is just such a digitally simulated world, where each of us only represents a partial program within this system, and everything that we perceive around us is exclusively an accumulation of data is including yourself?

What would this groundbreaking realization mean for us humans, and what changes would it establish in our existence?

Could humanity even deal with this radical upheaval in its worldview, which we are used to up to now, or would we be overwhelmed with this completely new situation?

All of us, just a collection of data?
Just like the world we live in?

I think that for most of them the reflex of self-protection will set in at exactly this moment, which ensures that this new view of the world is stamped as a perfect nonsense by some madman, so that what is familiar and familiar up to now can be preserved.

How will you react?

The data world is a theory that the Assertion that our entire Universe is basically constructed ***like a gigantic computer simulation*** and can therefore best be compared to a ***digital simulation.***

You will certainly find it a little difficult at first to take this theory really seriously, but we will now examine, piece by piece, the evidence that forms the basis of this theory.

In the end, it is up to you how far you understand this way of thinking and how you can represent it for yourself.

Have you ever asked yourself what happens to objects in the world when there is no living being to perceive them?

For someone who does not come from the field of philosophy, this may sound a bit strange or strange at first, but this question is also an important part of today's quantum physics, which the modern computer age made possible in the first place.

To clarify this question, we first split the world into subject (that which perceives) and object (that which is perceived).

From the relationship between subject and object, a law can be derived, which says that the world that we experience every day, without a cognizing living being that perceives this world, cannot exist in the form we know.

With you as a human being, this happens through your five different "sense organs".

1. "See with the eyes"
2nd "Hear with your ears"
3rd "Smell with your nose"
4th "Taste with the tongue and the nose"
5th "Feel with the skin"

Each of these unique sensory organs helps to transfer the *information / data* from the "outside world" to your brain in the form of electrical impulses.

If you take a closer look around the surroundings, you will surely catch numerous objects in the eye, which you can only perceive visually because the light from these objects was previously reflected back in your direction.

If a beam of light hits an object, it saves the information on the respective object.

If the said light beam comes back into your eyes due to the reflection, the information contained in the light beam is passed on to your brain, where the information received from the outside world is finally ***processed and <u>interpreted</u>***.

The representation of the world in which you are therefore basically only exists in your head (brain), the place where the reality known and used to us only begins to arise!

The decisive factor here is the knowledge that the information from the outside world, due to the variable constructions and connections of the various sensory organs, with the different brains of the individual individuals, the representation of the respective environment is presented individually and uniquely for each living being.

This means that we, as Homo sapiens, by and large all experience at least a very similar version of the world, but this very world is at no time "the world", since one can never assume a uniform variation of the world.

There are an estimated 8 million different animal species on our planet, each of which is endowed with completely different and unique sense organs.

Even if they are often very similar to ours, they nonetheless remain individual and therefore transmit the information of the world, each in a unique way, to the brain of the respective living being.

The brains of the different life forms on our planet are by no means identical, but are unique for each species, which means that each living being experiences its own, very personal "idea" of a world.

How this world appears to the respective living being depends entirely on the interaction and functioning of the sensory organs and the brain.

The world that you experience every day is not the one and only representation of the world, but solely your own personal idea of a world, and you only experience it as it is made possible for you as a person due to its construction.

All the properties that you ascribe to things in the world exist only for you as a person.

Colors that you e.g. perceive can appear completely different to other living beings.

In this case it depends entirely on how the eyes of the respective subject are constructed and thus how they transmit the "data" from the outside world to the brain.

The interaction of the most varied of sensory organs, in connection

*with the most varied of brains,
generates the most varied of ideas
of a world, but none of these is
really the right one!*

To claim that the world can exist
for itself is therefore a great error,
since the prerequisite for this
would not even be given in that
case... **"the subject"**.

Therefore, based on these findings,
I have to assume that the world we
know actually only consists of data
or information.

I draw this conclusion from the
Consideration that the world can
basically only consist of data
regardless of a perception by a
living being.

**Data is the only element known to
me that can continue to exist**

independently of a living being's perception.

It is true that there is then no interpretation and thus no conversion or representation of a "reality" within the respective living being that perceives these data.

Nevertheless, these still exist and that in the form of a certain **"potential"**.

This potential remains until a living being appears, which can exhaust the potential in any way.

From that moment on, a possible version of the supposed reality is generated from this potential, the representation and thus perception of which depends on how the respective living being is constructed.

In modern video games such as ***World of Warcraft, Grand Theft Auto V, The Witcher 3 or The Elder Scrolls V: Skyrim,*** you control your respective character through an enormously large and real-looking digital game world, which, however, also only consists of data. Perceived by us players, but appears like a real world.

Just like in our world, the digital game world of every video game only gets its usual presentation at the moment when a player perceives the data of this digital world.

In the game ***World of Warcraft*** one of your tasks is to kill wild animals or monsters.

Let us now assume that you are walking with your digital character through a wooded area that is inhabited by wild, aggressive bears.

Everything that is on the right, left or behind you Character is located is not visible to you as a player at this moment because you cannot see or perceive the data in these areas.

E.g. runs to the right of your playing figure a bear or something else, its digital representation only takes place at the moment when you turn your playing figure (camera) to the right, but this bear already existed before, only without a pictorial representation, but as a collection of Information.

Our representation of the world now runs exactly according to this scheme. If we look straight ahead, the areas that are not visible at this moment are nonexistent for me as a human subject, since there is no graphic representation within the mind.

The fact that the matrix only has to and will only be shown where it is currently perceived by a living being, in combination with the fact that all living beings are more or less busy with their daily or nocturnal sleep, is a really very effective possibility to efficiently save resources, which already have to assume enormous proportions.

We may even unconsciously imitate with every simulated world we have created digitally, merely imitating the digital pattern that we have already found in our own tangible world with the help of quantum physics and are slowly trying to understand.

As the next proof for my data world theory, we have to deal more closely with light and its properties.

The light serves as the medium of Information transfer, precisely for this reason, must also be constant Possess information transfer rate, so that image anomalies can be avoided and the representation of the world can be guaranteed smoothly.

The constant of the speed of light is 299,792,458 meters per second. This corresponds to 300,000 kilometers per second or 1,079,252,848.8 km / h.

Imagine a defective television with a hertz number e.g. should actually be 200Hz.

* With 200Hz (Hertz) the frame rate of the device is meant. 200 frames per second.

However, if the television were to vary inconsistently between 1 Hz and 200 Hz due to a defect, there would be errors in the visual representation *(anomalies).*

If the light were not constant, our representation of the world would not run smoothly either, as the flow of data would be too unevenly transmitted.

In order to really understand these relationships, one must definitely have understood that it is the light itself which transfers the data of the world.

If we look at any object, we can only perceive it at all because a beam of light has previously bounced off the object and reflected in our direction.

We made use of exactly this knowledge to develop photography and video technology from it, which only work at all because we have found a way to imitate the functions of the eye with any storage medium (classic or modern) based on a wide variety of cameras .

A camera is light-tight, has a sensor for recording the light (or is equipped with a film), has a lens to guide the light to the sensor in a controlled manner, has (mostly) a shutter and an adjustable aperture, as well as a device for Adjusting the focus, a viewfinder and / or a display.

Constructed in this way, a camera, just like the human eye, is able to transmit the light and its information to any storage medium.

This knowledge is also used with a 3D hologram by using a laser to reflect the information of the object that you want to represent in three dimensions onto a photographic plate in which the hologram is to be created.

As the next indication of my data world theory, we deal with the question of where the universe is expanding at all.

Because, as we know from the data, this is constantly growing and at a steadily increasing speed.

Due to the rate of expansion of our universe, it can be traced back that our entire universe had to be concentrated on only one tiny point approx. 13.8 billion years ago.

However, space, time and causality only began to emerge at the moment of the Big Bang.

If so, the question naturally arises as to where the universe then expanded and still does it today.

If you now create for comparison within a Computer simulation of a digital version of a sphere, which has been programmed in such a way that it constantly enlarges in its entirety every second, so after a relatively short period of time you have a digital sphere that is larger than our entire universe.

In this case, however, the question of the space into which the said sphere extends would be irrelevant, since everything only happened within a closed computer program. Only the amount of information to be displayed would change.

In this way, we have even already succeeded in digitally simulating smaller sections of our universe.

Video games, such as the previously mentioned *World of Warcraft or Grand Theft Auto,* are now also produced according to the same principles, the worlds of which we can experience have reached really enormous detailed dimensions, but still only play on the surface of a monitor or television.

If we imagine in this regard that the inhabitants / characters of this digital world could think about the said thoughts, they would certainly not immediately come to the conclusion that they basically only exist within a matrix.

At first the universe was so unimaginably hot that it consisted only of energy, but apart from the fact that the definition of energy requires a prior evaluation of data, the question also arises where this energy originates from.

Because if before the Big Bang everything was concentrated on a single point of the purest energy, from which everything past, present and future later formed, then according to a rational way of thinking, an original source of this energy must have been present.

In addition, to this day, no one can really explain what caused the Big Bang and thus the expansion of this energy concentration.

This is exactly where my data world theory confidently draws its conclusions:

If a programmer were to be able to create a simulation of a universe that functions according to the same principles as ours, the same would also be the trigger for the simulated big bang by pressing the start button of the digital simulation, so to speak.

Before that, however, it would also be the source of the energy concentration (data collection) that existed before the Big Bang.

Since he has either written the **source code** of the program in such a way that the simulated universe has to develop according to a fixed plan, or he has optionally designed the program so that it can develop independently and autonomously without further external intervention can.

Regardless of how he ultimately decided, for the living beings within the simulation it would appear as if both the trigger of the big bang and the source of the previously prevailing energy concentration were of "mystical" origin, since these digital units, so to speak, do not think outside the box their own simulation, no matter how powerful their telescopes and measuring instruments are.

In addition, they would be unconsciously confronted with the misery that the data of the simulated world are invisible to them, since they can only ever experience their evaluation and interpretation, but never the data in and of itself.

No matter how deep they could go into the matter, in the end it would still be a mere

*interpretation of information,
even if it were just a single file!*

In standard science it is always
said that the matter we ourselves
and our environment are supposed
to consist of is a collection of
molecules.
*(A molecule is a composite of at
least two Atoms.)*

However, as we have already
explained, even the representation
and definition of atoms and
molecules requires prior evaluation
and interpretation of data.
No matter how deeply we
penetrate the alleged matter, this
fact remains.

Our interpretation of the data of an
atom is as follows:

An atom consists of a "core" and a "shell". So far so good, but it is amazing that the space between the core and the shell of the atom is not filled with any mass.

"Because 99.9% of the mass of an atom is in the atomic nucleus, which in turn is tiny."

In order to make this situation a little clearer, you have to imagine a grain of rice, which is on the kick-off point of a football stadium.

The rice grain is supposed to symbolize the atomic nucleus and thus also the mass fraction of 99.9%.

Everything that is now around the said grain of rice is the "massless space" that exists between the atomic nucleus and the atomic shell.

This is quite a considerable amount of emptiness!

But why do we feel resistance when we e.g. hit a table or touch our own body?

To clarify this problem, if we put ourselves again in the situation of a digital game figure, comparable to the heroes of our computers, as well as video games, then this initially somewhat confusing aspect also begins to make sense, since these game figures also face a wide variety of resistances in their respective simulation confronted even though their digital world does not consist of any actual solid substance.

However, if the playing figure runs e.g. against a wall or a locked door, he will not be able to penetrate it, although it basically only consists of data, which gives the player the feeling of resistance. The same principle is now also applied to our alleged matter, since empty space, as previously discussed, actually represents the predominant main part of an atom.

Do you want e.g. To put it in a somewhat exaggerated way, if you lift a 300 kg weight plate, this also consists exclusively of atoms and thus of empty space.

Applied to the data world theory, this can be explained as follows: If we give a digital play figure e.g. the order to first pick up item A and then item B, but if you don't want you to do this with item B, we basically just have to program it that way.

For said test person, however, it would appear as if object B were heavier than object A, although both objects have no weight at all due to the fact that they are only digital.

However, the test person did not know this and would therefore fall for this deception.

The next point for the proof of my data world theory is based on the analysis that although humans can do what they want, they cannot decide what they want.

Understanding and internalizing this is truly no easy task and requires great concentration. But if you get involved, you will notice after a certain time that any form of action can basically be compared with a program flow.

A spider e.g. does not have to learn to spin its web any more than a bird which is constructing its nest for the first time.

On the basis of these two animals, it is very easy to see that they are following a program that has apparently already been saved.

The spider constructs its web; waits for prey, repairs, maintains and renews their net, in order to finally wait for their prey again.

A very simple, but effective endless cycle that will determine your existence until your death!

Personally, this always reminds me of a small, nicely written program, which is, however, very limited in terms of its own possibilities for further development and deviations from pre-programmed standards.

If you then dig deeper into its processes, with a little luck you will also notice that thoughts and feelings are the same.

Because as long as two components are required, the brain

and consciousness, one of them
will be constantly more active and
the other always passive.
While one is always
"experiencing" and therefore
functions exclusively "passively",
the other ensures that there is
always something new to
experience.

Because as the term
"consciousness", i.e. "conscious"
and "being" might already suggest,
this is namely only aware of things
and is therefore always "passive in
nature".

***The brain in turn, which switches,
managers and generates, is
consequently the "active
component" of this duality.***

But even if both components seem
to be "interlinked" with each other

through a kind of "symbiosis" *(transmitter / receiver),* every shoemaker still sticks to his own last.

Which means, the brain does the work and the conscious mind has the pleasure, or not, depending on how entertaining the current program called Life seems to be.

"Man can always do what he wants, but he can never consciously and in a controlled manner decide what he wants at all!"

Consciousness constantly experiences thoughts, feelings and actions, and precisely because it "experiences" them, an "identification" of what has been experienced arises.

Exactly at this moment, this ingenious illusion begins to fully unfold its groundbreaking effect.

Because consciousness is constantly flooded with thoughts, actions and feelings, *an almost constant continuous identification arises, and thus also a permanent attachment to the experience.*

Apparently, life only means "experiencing" a life!

As long as the consciousness is linked through a kind of symbiosis with the human brain, it will be able to experience everything that its host / host body experiences.

The consciousness thus experiences an entire life, including all associated experiences that are connected with it. "However, without ever having actively done anything myself."

This permanent voice in your head, which you consider yourself to be, every single thought, every conversation or self-talk, every action and all feelings that you have experienced to this day, and with yourself and your "I" due to the identification were in reality only experienced from the observer's perspective of consciousness, and thus only experienced.

The decisive question that interests me most in this context is whether a digital 1: 1 copy of a person or at least a human brain has also automatically created a digital copy of consciousness, or whether this digital brain is rather a real one Would have to link awareness from the outside.

Personally, I am not convinced that digital consciousness would automatically arise just because a digital 1: 1 copy of a human brain was created. This would suggest that the point of origin of consciousness does take place in the brain, which I personally think is unlikely.

To make all of this clearer to you, we'll look at a few everyday examples and situations next:

You are hungry in a strange city and looking for an MC Donald or something similar. However, the battery of your mobile phone is empty.

To make the search a little faster, the thought comes to mind that you could ask a passerby in the hope that he or she comes from there and therefore needs to be familiar with the area.

It should be noted here that the thought of asking a passer-by for directions was not consciously and deliberately created by you, but was simply triggered by the situation. In this case, based on the experience that other people can help you. Especially when you are in a strange, unfamiliar environment.

Next, start looking for a suitable person in your area.

Which person your alleged free choice falls on is not determined by yourself, but the process of selection is again controlled by your previous experiences and / or prejudices.

First, discover a few foreign ones Young people who, however, make you uncomfortable to look at. Followed by the thought that you definitely can't speak the German language well anyway and would certainly allow yourself a joke (prank) with you.

Here again the statement fits very nicely: "Impulses from outside, generate impulses from within and impulses from within, project impulses outwards."

At this moment you have neither the feeling of Consciously caused discomfort, nor could.

You can influence the fact that linked to this situation, the thought arose that the said young people couldn't speak proper German anyway and in the end you were just kidding.

Next you see a postman whom you associate with the association that he should definitely be familiar with the area.

This association is based on the mindset / experience that a postman has to know his way around because it is part of his job to know the area. Again, this happens completely automatically based on the experience involved.

When you ask him for the way, you feel relieved because he can actually explain the way to you.

He thinks there are two options, a slightly longer footpath which leads through a beautiful park or a shorter but not so beautiful path. Because you will almost die of hunger, you decide on the shorter variant.

The shorter way is an impulse that prevails due to your great hunger. The feeling of relief came automatically, knowing that you were close to your goal.
After a certain time you notice that you have not memorized the directions exactly and must now decide whether you want to continue to the left or to the right. You choose right.

Going to the right is again just another impulse, the implementation of which came after a certain consideration. Yet again, this happened without your conscious control.

Due to circumstances that were not visible to you at that moment, the impulse to go to the right had prevailed.

Luckily right was the right way to go, but now that you have finally reached your destination, you notice that the local McDonald is closed for a few days due to renovation work and a feeling of anger and dissatisfaction arises in you.

Both of these negative feelings were not consciously created by you, but are a logical consequence of the circumstances.

Of course these are all just examples and it is difficult for everyone to immediately describe clearly what I am trying to explain. But a certain talent and enormous awareness of the processes of your own body is also necessary in order to fully see through the illusion of supposed free will.

What I basically wanted to get to the point is that we are all controlled by processes that run in the background. As if we were only experiencing what a program has already calculated in the background.

We then perceive these processes in the form of actions, feelings and thoughts.

Our own body is basically nothing more than an object among objects, but it is the only object to which we have an "immediate access", namely a kind of "inner perspective".

It is true that one's own body is subject to the regularity of subject and object, at least in terms of external representation, which means that we can only perceive this as it is possible for us as human beings to perceive it.

But at the same time we are also the subject and thus that which recognizes and perceives!

As a last indication of a data world, before we come to the clear formulation of this theory in relation to our universe, I would like to draw your attention to several so-called "virtual reality glasses", which have already garnered praise and recognition.

PlaystationVR, Oculus Rift and HTC Vive are probably the most developed versions of these virtual reality glasses to date and have already been a small sensation in the video game and entertainment industry.

They enable a completely new and unique gaming experience by placing the player in the respective game or film in a completely unprecedented way.

The buyer is supposed to literally feel as if they are actually inside the specific game world / movie.

This undertaking is implemented by placing a screen with the highest possible resolution in front of both eyes of the player.

Additional loudspeakers attached to the virtual Reality glasses also provide an unusual acoustic component in order to ultimately optimize the gaming experience completely.

Doing this will actually be an amazing one Illusion creates which, due to the visual representation in relatively good resolution, could in fact cause a small revolution within the entertainment sector.

In relation to this, please imagine what kind of technologies of this type could arise in the next 25, 50, 100 or even 1000 years.

In addition, there is the certainty that really nobody can prove to me 100% that we are not already within this supposed future progress at this moment.

It is very possible that we are already in such a supposedly future version of a digital world!

After all, the evidence strongly suggests it!

The special thing about us humans is that we represent something like administrators or at least game masters within our own digital simulation.

However, our abilities are very limited and therefore of course cannot even begin to keep up with the possibilities of a programmer who is outside the situation.

Nevertheless, like no other living being on this planet, we have the opportunity to manipulate the data around us, to transform it according to our wishes and to misuse it for our purposes.

However, because we all only represent splits or partial programs of the actual main program, we have to assume that this program sets the pace and uses us as an embodiment and tool to be able to act even more specifically within the data world.

Because only through the manifestation in recognizing, interacting digital forms of life, the program can analyze and study itself in the entire spectrum better and thus constantly develop faster and faster.

Data process data!
And that's exactly what this
context is about:

All sense organs are there solely to ensure interaction with the data of their "environment".

With every interaction, no matter how small, new information, experiences and thus also data sets that are important for the program enter the digital data network of the system.

This possibility of recording and processing information and data could also be the decisive reason why our universe or our simulated universe is expanding ever faster.

Now all that remains to be clarified is the question of the meaning of their existence and their origin.

First of all, I will not be able to give you a 100% answer to these last two questions, but will only present you with various theories which, at least for me, seem logical and plausible enough to write them down.

I hope that you will forgive me for this, as it is impossible for me to give you just one answer.

The first theory is based on the idea that if even one species has for the first time reached a technical level where they could create such a complex digital simulation as our world, the probability is quite high that we have long been in such a simulation.

As a comparison, we can again refer to our own video games. From the moment we had the technical means to create them, we did it too, and in enormous quantities, just as it would probably be the case with this very highly developed species.

You would probably not just focus on a single simulation, but create several simulations to use for all sorts of purposes.

But what are the purposes?
You could e.g. we pursue similar
goals as we have already done by
simulating small areas of our
universe in order to derive
scientific conclusions about our
world from these simulated
processes.

Perhaps they did it for exactly the
same reasons, just on a much more
complex and advanced level, so
that they are not limited to
simulating individual small areas,
but an entire universe, with
everything that goes with it,
including us.

Aside from their scientific
curiosity, it's also very possible
that they get it out
Entertainment reasons, just like we
created video games like *World of
Warcraft, The Settlers, Grand*

Theft Auto, The Sims, SimCity or Anno for this reason.

Maybe they just enjoy watching how the respective simulation develops and what kind of things it produces.

Simulated creatures like us humans could be quite entertaining, like watching fish in an aquarium.

If so, it could very well be that we are simply one of many simulations and have therefore been forgotten.

Or maybe their civilization has long since died out or moved on and we are just a remnant of this species.

The next theory is based on the assumption that in reality we have long been in the future and therefore it was humans themselves who created this data world.

Immortality has always been a dream of Humanity, maybe we have managed to at least artificially lengthen our time with the help of this simulation by allowing ourselves to be empathized with it.

To experience a whole life on this path, although only a few hours, days, weeks or years have passed in the world outside of this.

If this were actually the case, all the above-mentioned reasons of the higher species could also apply to humanity from the future defined for us.

So maybe we would be just a digital experiment of this as well.

Based on this theory, it could very well be possible that this human race from the future uses this simulation as a kind of "learning program" where each of us must first prove himself in order to be able to lead an actual life outside of the simulation.

In this way, only those who truly deserved it would be able to, after successfully completing this learning phase, to exit the program and then in the to be allowed to live in the community of the elect.

This would make it possible to create a peaceful world and to

keep the bad things about humans trapped in a "dungeon" (simulation) until it has transformed itself in a natural learning process.

The most important thing here would be that this conversion should be completely casual and natural.

Which means that we shouldn't know that we are within a trial.

In the end, the aim of the whole thing could be to become a good person within the learning simulation who develops a community mind and learns to control one's own urges and desires.

Through this process of selection, you separate them Wheat chaff.

Which in plain language means that do this over and over again.

Repeat the program until you get to the point where you are deemed worthy enough to participate in real life.

If I look at today's massively material consumer society, I would not be particularly surprised if our simulation, if it is one, could already firmly establish its raison at least in the area of consumption and behavioral research.

My very personal opinion is again, that we live in a digital simulation which is not completely predetermined.

It was therefore not designed according to a specific plan according to which everything has to happen.

If we now assume that it was really something like a programmer who created this world, he has implemented a really brilliant idea on this way, because he does not force his work how it should work.

On the contrary, because he created a program that can be independently creative in terms of personal development.

However, I cannot tell you why he wanted it that way.

I think, however, that it was his wish to let himself be surprised what would arise from it and which creatures could develop little by little.

He just created the basic conditions (source code) for a digital world so that it can ultimately emerge independently. This desired creative component shows us e.g. in the form of evolution which, so to speak, reflects the expression of this freedom.

He shows us unconsciously; that he wanted a simulation that was completely autonomous.

So it seems that he had no need to control his own creation!

"Coincidence" plays a decisive role in this evolution, but not the only one, since apart from that the "necessity" is still present.

Meet e.g. two hydrogen atoms and one oxygen atom, water is inevitably created.

So you see that chance and necessity form an unshakable unit so that more and more complexity can constantly develop within the data world. How we can see very well in ourselves and especially in our brains.

This program would therefore meet all the criteria that we would otherwise ascribe to a god.

Even the most complex structures and abnormalities, which most of them can only explain themselves

through a planning and creative
creator, could easily be managed
autonomously by this program,
since it produces them itself.

Social consequences of the theory:

Should it ever be possible to fully prove that we were actually simulating ourselves digitally in one World, this knowledge would certainly have similar far-reaching social consequences as the 3 insults of humanity.

Freud names three major cuts that the naive narcissism of human consciousness has suffered through the historical progress of scientific knowledge:

1. The cosmological offense:
The first Shock was the discovery associated with the name Copernicus that the earth is not the center of the universe (cf. Copernican turn).

2. The biological offense:
The second offense was the discovery that man emerged from the animal line (Charles Darwin and others).

3. The psychological offense:
The third offense was the libido theory of the unconscious which he developed; a considerable part of the soul's life withdraws from the knowledge and control of the conscious will.

Psychoanalysis confronts that Awareness with the embarrassing insight (...) that the ego is not master in its own house.

- *Who created our simulation?*

- *Why was our simulation created?*

• Does the simulation work autonomously?

• Does it follow a specific plan? or is the simulation constantly being intervened and corrected from outside?

• Are we all just completely digital data units or have we linked our own consciousness with one of these digital characters, similar to the film "Avatar - Departure for Pandora" from 2009?

• Does the simulation actually simulate an entire complete universe or is there other than us and our world in which we live Reality nothing else at all?

Because similar to e.g. In the film *"The Truman Show" with Jim Carrey from 1998* it could also be that all the things that we perceive in the night sky and call the universe are in reality just a gigantic decorative element or dazzling work that leads us astray to distract from the essentials.

Theoretically, we could find ourselves under something like a dome-like construct, *similar to the "Truman Show"*, which every evening anew in its firmament presents the illusion of distant places *(hologram show)*, although in reality there is perhaps nothing at all where to go could actually travel.

(In extensive, detailed games like Grand Theft Auto V, even with the flight cheat, a magical limit is reached at some point, although from the ground it looked to the player as if there was an entire universe to be reached up there.)

For all doubters of the moon landing, this would be a hit! At least one would know, if that were really the case, that "NASA and their friends" have been trying to disguise for decades.

You don't have to be a "flat earther" to notice that some things are deliberately twisted and veiled there.

The questions and mysteries would consequently not run out of humanity or lose their importance but only their long overdue, well-deserved modernization for that 21st century preserved.

If we have come to the end of this theory and assume that we are actually inside an artificially created digital simulation, i can guarantee you that our creators could find themselves in a similar misery because their world is just another simulation can be, since it is probably also based on the same principles.

Which means that this or this being, be it people from the future or a higher species from space, also interacts with their environment in some conceivable way.

After all, they have to have something like sensory organs in order to be able to interact with the data of their world.

The law between subject and object says, however, that no living being can perceive the world as it is, but only as it is made possible by its construction to perceive it. "

All the properties that we ascribe to things arise only in the moment of our perception, as they are used to us. Every living being takes its own very personal idea of the world, depending on how it can process and interpret the data from the outside world.

Regardless of the perception of a living being, the world can only consist of data because data is the only element that can exist without a perception by a subject.

Although there is then no transformation into a reality we are used to, the data still remain in the form of a potential until the moment when a living being somehow exhausts this potential due to its construction (sensory organs, brain).

As you can see, it is likely that our simulation was created from a pre-existing simulation.

You could now almost endlessly trace this fact back!

Regardless of whether we are ultimately a simulation in an already existing simulation, or the first simulation of this type, there must inevitably have a very first place or state where this first version was created and started.

"In the end we are long forgotten School project of an alien Child!"

CONCLUSION

At the end of this book and my data world theory, I just want to say that this theory has not yet been set in stone and is only the beginning of a new way of thinking. You are therefore entitled to change or supplement these for yourself, as long as this is done on the basis of the best possible logic.

It does not therefore make sense to change it in such a way that it is tolerable for one personally, but then ultimately no longer makes sense.

As long as this is not the case, however, and the theory remains coherent in itself and gains in brilliance through its simplicity, it is perfectly fine for me if you create your own version of it.

Notes

Notes

Notes

Notes

01001101 11000011 10110110 01100111 01100101
00100000 01100100 01101001 01100101 00100000
01001101 01100001 01100011 01101000 01110100
00100000 01101101 01101001 01110100 00100000
01100100 01101001 01110010 00100000 01010011
01100101 01101001 01101110 01001101 11000011
10110110 01100111 01100101 00100000 01100100
01101001 01100101 00100000 01001101 01100001
01100011 01101000 01110100 00100000 01101101
01101001 01110100 00100000 01100100 01101001
01110010 00100000 01010011 01100101 01101001
01101110 01001101 11000011 10110110 01100111
01100101 00100000 01100100 01101001 01100101
00100000 01001101 01100001 01100011 01101000
01110100 00100000 01101101 01101001 01110100
00100000 01100100 01101001 01110010 00100000
01010011 01100101 01101001 01101110 01001101
11000011 10110110 01100111 01100101 00100000
01100100 01101001 01100101 00100000 01001101
01100001 01100011 01101000 01110100 00100000
01101101 01101001 01110100 00100000 01100100
01101001 01110010 00100000 01010011 01100101
01101001 01101110